BATIK:
THE ART AND
CRAFT

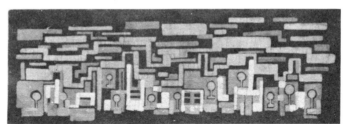

BATIK:
THE ART
AND
CRAFT

By ILA KELLER

CHARLES E. TUTTLE COMPANY: PUBLISHERS   Rutland, Vermont & Tokyo, Japan

Representatives

For Continental Europe:
BOXERBOOKS, INC., *Zurich*

For the British Isles:
PRENTICE-HALL INTERNATIONAL, INC., *London*

For Australasia:
PAUL FLESCH & CO., PTY. LTD., *Melbourne*

For Canada:
M.G. HURTIG, LTD., *Edmonton*

Published by the Charles E. Tuttle Company, Inc.
of Rutland, Vermont and Tokyo, Japan
with editorial offices at
Suido 1-chome, 2–6
Bunkyo-ku, Tokyo, Japan

Copyright in Japan, 1966 by Charles E. Tuttle Co., Inc.

Library of Congress Catalog Card No. 66–16267

Standard Book No. 8048 0059-6

First printing, 1966
Fifth printing, 1970

Book design and typography by John Paull
Printed in Japan

BATIK or "wax writing"
as the Javanese translate it,
has become my medium and code
for communication with many people
of many distant places

Table of Contents

Table of Contents

List of Illustrations

MODERN BATIK METHOD

NOTE

Unless captioned otherwise, all examples illustrated are the work of the author.

My sincere thanks to all who contributed to this book, in particular; Ambassador Dr. and Mrs. Fred Bieri of Switzerland; The Cultural Counselor of the Indonesian Embassy, Washington D.C.; The Museum of Ethnology, Basel, Switzerland; The Röhsska Konstslöjdmuseet, Göteborg, Sweden; Mr. Grant Cole of Glens Fall, N.Y., for his photography, and last but not least, to my husband and son.

Acknowledgment

Acknowledgment is made to the following for permission to use illustrations included in this book.

Ambassador Fred Bieri, Swiss Embassy, Djarkarta: Figs. 11, 13, 15, 16, 19, 20. *Batiks from Java,* Royal Tropical Institute, Amsterdam: Figs. 4–10, 25. Embassy of Indonesia, Washington, D.C.: Figs. 12, 14, 17, 18. Museum fur Volkerkunde, Basel, Switzerland: Figs. 1–3. Röhsska Konstslöjdmuseet, Göteborg, Sweden: Fig. 62. Smithsonian Institute, Washington, D.C.: Fig. 58. Standard Oil (N.J.): Fig. 21.

Batik is so old a craft that its true origin has never been determined, but it can safely be presumed to be at least 2,000 years old. Archaeological findings prove that the people of Egypt and Persia used to wear batiked garments, and the same can be said of the people of India, China, Japan, and most countries in the East. In Africa, batik occurs in the symmetrical tribal patterns; in India, in the ancient paisley pattern; and in China and Japan it has lent itself perfectly to delicate Oriental designs.

There are many theories to explain the possible origin of batik, though none leaves us completely without doubt. If it originated in Egypt, it may easily have spread to Africa and Persia and subsequently all the way to the East, adapting itself to the individual touch of each nation. In contrast, J. A. Loeber states in his book on batik, *Das Batiken, eine Blute des indonesischen Kunstlebens,* that it is more likely to have originated in the Indian Archipelago. History tells of people of that area wearing white clothes, dyeing them blue as they became dirty, and discarding them only when they had shredded into rags. The natives of Flores used rice starch to extend the lifetime of their clothes, and since we know for sure that rice starch was the fore-runner of wax in the development of batik, Mr. Loeber's theory is certainly supported by quite a few facts.

THE HISTORY OF BATIK

1 *Man's smock. African batik on cotton*

2 *Cotton batik. Pa-Miao tribe. China*

Wherever we turn in search of that ancient craft, we always seem to lose the trail in the mist of unrecorded history. Some archaeological findings of batiks trace back to the 10th century. Ruins of a temple on Java dating back to about the 13th century show fragments of stone figures wearing garments decorated with motifs strongly resembling the sarong of the 20th century in style and decoration. On the grounds of this evidence, by the 12th century batik had reached Java, where it established itself as an important part of Indonesian culture and economy.

In the book, *Arts and Crafts in Indonesia,* (Ministry of Information, Djakarta) the word "batik," as such, is derived from *ambatik,* meaning a cloth of little dots. A "little bit" or a "little dot" means *tik,* which once again resembles the Javanese word *tritic* or *taritic.*

At first, batik was applied to homemade cottons and calico but with Marco Polo and probably even before him, some fine muslin reached the Oriental bazaars. The finely woven quality of this cloth was perfect for batik as well as the climate.

As each house of aristocracy has its coat of arms and each clan of Scotland its own tartan, so the nobility of Java introduced their own motifs and colors. According to the book *The Art of Batik,* (R. Soeprapto) Sultan Hanjokrikusmo, who ruled from 1613 to 1645, was very fond of the craft and created many beautiful and deeply symbolic designs.

At first batik was merely a pastime of the ladies of the Javanese courts, but it became a matter of social status to wear batiked *sarongs* to display one's artistry in design and color. In order to keep the wardrobes well stocked, all ladies of the court were soon engaged in the decoration of their robes. As time passed, the ladies-in-waiting and even the servants had to give a helping hand, and batik continued to grow in popularity. It had become a national costume worn by men and women alike.

All the natural things surrounding the Javanese, such as birds, flowers, fruits, foliage, butterflies, fish, and shells, were used in the most elaborate motifs to embellish their sarongs, *kains, kembangs,* and *slendangs*. Religious law, however, forbids the Moslem to represent any living being, so the peacock and eagle, those very royal creatures, and the elephant and all other animals had to be stylized to obey that provision. There were hundreds of patterns,

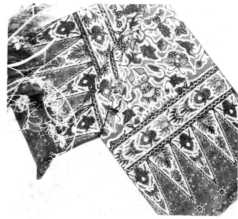

3 *Batik Kemban with ornamental spider border*

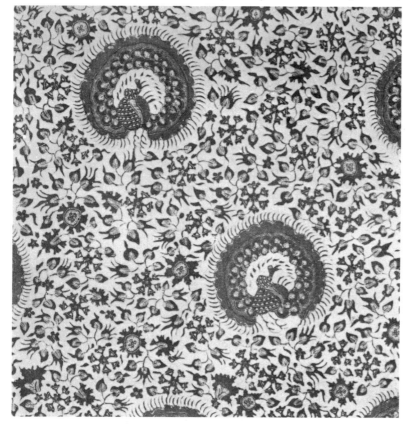

Basic Patterns

4 *Stylised peacock pattern from Semarang*

many of which assumed their own names and withstood the changes of time and outside influence for centuries. Principal basic patterns are the *kawung, parang, tjeplok,* and *semen.*

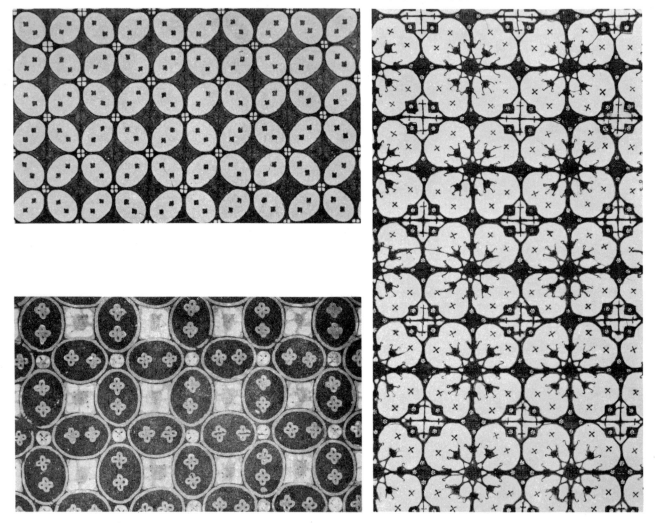

Basic Kawung Patterns

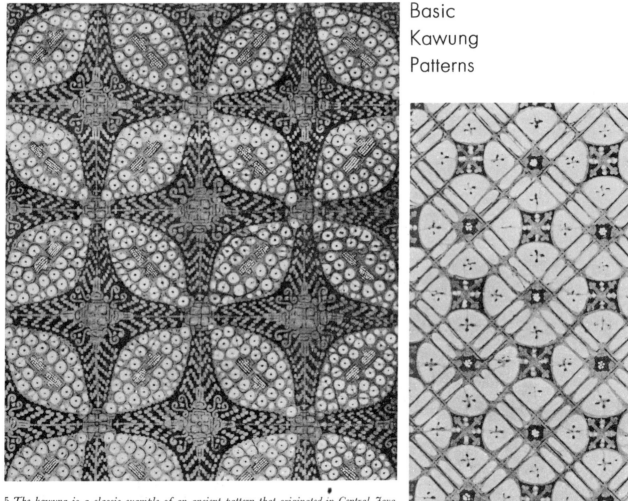

5 *The kawung is a classic example of an ancient pattern that originated in Central Java. According to the natives, the ovals in the design represent the fruit of the* kapok *tree, the* areng *leaf, and the like. The characteristic of the kawung pattern is the arrangement of the ovals or ellipses in groups of four, embellished with tiny floral motifs. The kawung can be traced back to 1239 A.D. when it appeared on a stone* ganeca *from Kediri*

Basic Parang Patterns

6 *The word 'parang' may be literally translated as 'rugged rock' or even 'chopping knife.' The pattern, which originated in Solo, central Java, can always be recognised by its diagonal craggy lines, or stripes, often with a scalloped border. The wider stripes contain small geometrical design of floral motif*

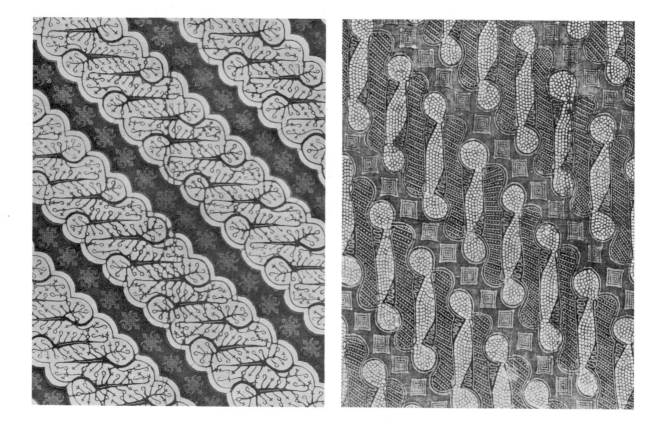

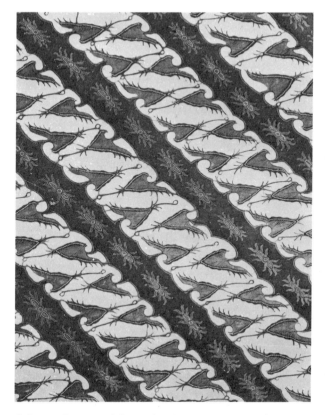

7 *Parang from central Java. This design is used on stoles worn by girl dancers*

8 *The light dots on the pattern are interlaced with a design derived from the kusumo flower. This is one of the patterns forbidden to commoners by royal decree*

Basic
Tjeplok
Patterns

9 *The tjeplok pattern is a continuous symmetrical pattern composed of stars, crosses, or rosettes, which form circles and squares. Any animals or flowers in the design are fitted into the geometrical arrangement*

10 *Young leaves or shoots are shown on a clear background, surrounded by stylized flora and fauna. Most semen patterns show non-Javanese influence*

Basic
Semen
Patterns

22

With the ever increasing trade and the Dutch sovereignty over Java in the 16th century, Javanese batiks were introduced to Holland and subsequently all of Europe. It became a challenging new subject for artists and craftsmen, and they successfully simplified the process. They had a few things in their favor, such as the invention of the aniline dyes and the development of dry cleaning, along with various gadgets and utensils which most of the Javanese could not afford. At the beginning of this century the Dutchmen Lebeau and Pieter Mijer produced some truly beautiful hangings. They worked with the brush and the *tjanting* (a cup with spout, holding the melted wax) and executed the most intricate designs with amazing skill and accuracy.

The artists Dijesselhof, Cachet, Slaughter, Shirtleff, Wedel, Arthur Crisp, Bertrand Hartmann, Ethelyn Stewart, and many more contributed a great deal to the henceforth unrecognized craft. The wax-drop resist technique of batik fascinated the artists who had so far been used to painting mainly with oil and water colors. The top fashion designers used batik to enhance and accentuate their creations as one way of obtaining material that made each gown an original.

With the light filtering through the fabric as it does in batiked lamp shades, screens, and partitions, batik is second only to stained glass in its brilliancy, but exceeds stained glass in its delicacy and variety of texture, characteristics which make it a favorite in interior decoration.

As with many of the fine arts and crafts, batik has also become subject to some imitations, in this case the machine-printed cottons falsely called batik because they have scraggly lines printed over the material, copying the crackle effect which is so characteristic of batik work.

In Europe, batik has been taught at academies of fine arts and crafts for at least forty or fifty years. The technique by now has become very different from the Indonesian one, but it has remained a fascinating craft, lasting and varied in its possibilities. Contemporary artists have come to recognize it as a pliable medium to underline the mood and expression of their work. In comparison with the fine arts of painting in oil or water color, batik has its limitations, but it also has many well defined advantages over the graphic arts. The artist or craftsman must be capable of visualizing a complete picture of his idea before he has undertaken the first step. Once the process has been started, it is practically impossible to correct any mistakes in drawing or dyeing.

11 *Tulis batik from Solo, Indonesia*

Nowadays batik dyes in Indonesia consist mostly of aniline dyes, but before these were available on the Indonesian market, the Javanese had successfully developed dyes of their own. Through rigorous methods they produced colors that faded very little, considering the rugged wear imposed by bathing, which the Javanese often enjoy fully dressed plus the strong sun and a humid climate. The production of these colors, however, was so complicated and tedious that it took little to convince them of the advantages offered by the new product, aniline dye. Thus aniline dyes have almost replaced the ancient vegetable dyes.

With the growing demand for batiked cloth, the men took over the dyeing of the fabrics, while the women carried on the designing and waxing of the fabrics in the age-old tradition.

Some Chinese settlers on the island started "batik factories" which involved whole villages in the production. The output of these "factories" bears strong Chinese influence in the design. For two reasons the Javanese prefer the finely-woven cotton muslins: they are easy to work with and pleasant to wear. Silk materials are used less frequently.

Before the application of the design, the fabric undergoes several washings to free it from starch, chalk, and any other sizing it may contain. Then it is soaked in coconut oil or *djarak* oil for a few

BATIK IN INDONESIA

12 *Javanese girls selling batiks*

days. This changes the clear white of the fabric to a creamy white and also acts as a color-fastening agent in the cloth. Excess oil is removed by boiling the cloth in water which contains rice stalk ashes. After this, the piece of material, cut to size and hemmed, is laid out in the sun to dry. It is restarched with rice water to keep the threads in place, dried again, and rolled up. The roll gets a good pounding from a wooden hammer or a stone to make the material soft and supple and to prevent the wax from spreading too freely into the fiber of the threads.

For the application of the design, or the waxing, the material is draped over an A-frame or a similar bamboo stand. On a charcoal fire sits an iron pan or a stone pot containing the molten wax, which generally consists of pure beeswax mixed with a little animal fat and a few grains of Borneo rosin. The wax is applied to both sides of the fabric with tjantings of various sizes and types, and in the case of larger areas, a dab of cotton tied to the end of a stick so it resembles a brush.

For example, a batik that will finally be cream-white, blue, red, and purple, the dyeing proceeds as follows.

All parts of the design that are to resist the blue dye are waxed first. This covers all that is to remain cream-white as well as the areas which will be dyed red at a later stage.

The fabric is then immersed in the blue dye, mainly indigo blue, and dried. Thus the material is now cream-white and blue, and with the next dyeing of red, two more colors are obtained, namely red and purple. To get the red, however, some of the waxed parts have to be exposed, and this is done by first peeling off the wax with a small knife and then sponging on hot water.

The piece then undergoes another starching in rice water, which contains *aren-sugar* and pulverized *randoe* leaves.

This time all areas that are to resist the red dye have to be

13 *Women wearing national costume*

waxed over, which means all the parts that are to remain cream-white and blue. The unprotected, or unwaxed, sections of blue will become purple in the red dye, and all that was cream-white will now be a brilliant red. The red dye would most likely be derived from *soga* bark.

Thus having obtained all the required colors, the piece of material is dipped in a solution of Java sugar, alum, and whiting which will add a delicate glow to the fabric and at the same time act as a fixative.

Finally the material is rinsed very thoroughly and transferred to a hot water bath. In this, the wax will melt away from the fabric and float to the top of the vat from where it is ladled and collected for further use, such as the waxing of dark colors.

With the wax removed, the completed design will now be exposed.

Should the design call for other color combinations or more colors, which vary from province to province, the whole procedure would be repeated. Taking into account the time essential for the dyeing, and even more for the application of the very elaborate designs, it is obvious that this process is very lengthy. Sometimes the making of a single *kain* (a piece of cloth two to three yards long and three yards wide) requires a period from five weeks to as much as six months or more.

14 *Costumes of West Java (Feudal Period)*

15 *Balinese women with flower offerings*

The Tjanting

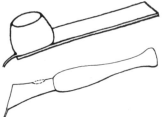

This is an instrument to apply the liquid wax to the fabric, and consists of a small copper reservoir with one or more spouts, affixed to a handle.

This small important tool has undergone many changes in a search for improvement, but artists have always returned to the same *tjanting* as it was seven hundred years ago in Java. The only change is that the handle is in a modern concept.

The *tjanting pengado* has twin spouts, and there are some tjantings with as many as six.

16 *Preserving the first color of a kain*

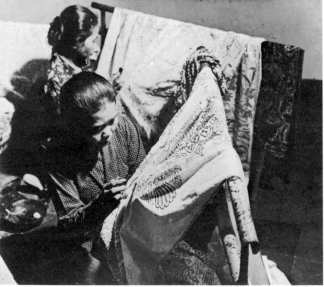

17 *Javanese women 'writing' the wax*

18 *Applying wax to a tulis batik*

19 *Workers at the Batik Co-operative Society, Solo*

20 *Young girl using the tjanting*

21 *Printing a batik with a tjap*

The *tjap* (a die used for repeating a pattern) has been used in Madras, India, since the 15th century according to the *Encyclopedia Britannica* (Editions 1957, 1959). However, the Javanese maintain that they invented the tjap in order to supply the poor with clothes closely resembling a batik, yet produced much more cheaply.

For a layman it would be difficult to distinguish between an authentic batik, which is also called a *tulis* batik and has been waxed with a tjanting, as against a tjap batik where the wax has been applied with a tjap. But to the Indonesian the difference stands out clearly, and no member of the upper class in Indonesia would dream of wearing a tjap.

The design in a tjap is quite repetitous and almost always shows some joints or seams in the pattern where the design has failed to match.

The method of printing is similar to block-printing, except that the tjap, or die, applies the wax instead of the color. Copper strips are arranged in a design and inserted in a block of wood, forming the tjap. Attached to the tjap is a handle.

A stamp-pad is made out of jute fiber wrapped in a muslin bag. This is thoroughly saturated with melted wax and kept hot in a skillet placed over a charcoal fire. The tjap is pressed on the pad, absorbing wax, and then applied to the fabric, leaving the design. This is repeated until the cloth is completely covered, giving an impression of a real batik, as executed with the tjanting.

In other words, it is a form of reproduction.

The procedure, carried out by men only, requires great accuracy and skill, especially when waxing the underneath of the cloth to marry with the design previously printed on the front.

The Tjap

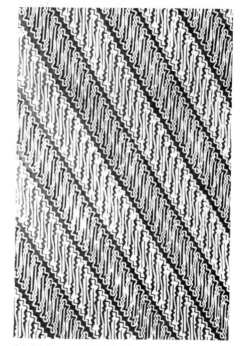

22 *Well executed tjap batik*

Language of Indonesian Fashion

SARONG: A piece of material between three to five yards long and about 40″ to 42″ wide. A garment worn by men and women alike, but twisted about the body in various ways.

SARONG KAPALA: A headdress consisting of a square piece of material worn chiefly by men, wound around the head like a turban, then taken off very carefully to be starched in this form.

KAIN PANDJANG: A sarong decorated with an all-over pattern for everyday wear.

KAIN KAPALA: A sarong for special occasions, with a more elaborate design and at one end, from selvedge to selvedge, decorated with a very intricate pattern called the *kapala*.

KEMBAN: A strip of material wound tightly around the chest, leaving shoulders and arms bare.

DODOT: Another type of kain, worn only at court. It can be draped around the body in various ways.

SLENDANG: A sort of stole, about three yards long and approximately 18″ wide, with a plain center and a decorative border or with an all-over design. It is worn by women over their heads, or used as a carry-all for babies as well as personal effects.

23 *Kain Kapala from Pekalongan*

Ancient Designs

Certain colors indicate that the wearer is a native of a particular part of Java or, in some cases, of noble descent. For example, some of the *parang* patterns (diagonal stripes with jagged borders) are to be worn by royalty only. The court of Jogjakarta and Solo had a definite preference for the deep indigo blues and the golden browns. For festive occasions some sarongs and kains are coated with gold dust on one side, and the batik workers of the north coast of central Java took a special fancy to this procedure. A concoction of linseed oil, a particular kind of incense, and some yellow earth make up the agglutinant and retain the tinge of gold even after laundering. The batiks of Pekalongan are rich and varied in color. The designs of the northern coast of central Java show pronounced European, Chinese, and Malayan influence.

Cream-white is usually the lightest shade in any garment. Clear white is rarely used because it signifies death or mourning, and mourning robes are never decorated at all.

24 *Kain demonstrating one of the parang patterns which are to be worn at official ceremonies only*

25 *The* wayang *(shadow dance) tells of datutkatjo, the son of Bima, who wore a patchwork jacket which enabled him to fly. This* tambul mireng *pattern is an imitation of that patchwork. It is only used for special garments, such as those worn by sultans and high priests. Central Java*

As with any of the arts and crafts, the basis for success is a aptitude for color and design, plus talent and skill. Other very important factors with batik are time and patience; natural elements in the East, but sadly lacking in the West. So if batik appeals to you but you are the forever-short-of-time type, do not get involved with this craft; the results will be far from satisfactory.

The attempt to simplify the technique has been successful to some extent, but it has failed whenever it has strayed too far from the fundamentals of the craft, for then batik is robbed of its characteristics.

An experienced artist can execute swift sketches in batik and be tremendously expressive. The same idea attempted by a beginner would most likely produce something hardly worthy of the name "batik." I therefore suggest a one-color batik for the start until you have acquired a feeling and understanding for the craft; only then can you successfully exploit your imagination for future projects.

In batik we achieve a greater harmony of color than in painting, due to the fact that each color is dyed over the previous one, and in this manner they become more closely related.

The fun is in experimenting and exploring all the possibilities of this craft, possibilities which I feel I have not yet exhausted.

MODERN BATIK METHOD

26 *Batik by Gosta Sandberg*

Western Techniques

List of Utensils

Wooden Frame or Stretcher
Fabric
Wax
Hotplate or Burner
Brushes or Tjanting
Dye Vat
Pan or Double boiler

Immersable Thermometer
Dyes
Rubber Gloves
Iron
Ironing Board
Absorbent Paper

27 *Utensils for making a batik*

Supplies of wax, dyes, tjantings, stretchers, etc. can be obtained from:

Suppliers

CRAFTOOLS INC.
1 Industrial Road
Wood-Ridge, New Jersey 07075

ALJO MANUFACTURING CO.
116 Prince Street
New York, New York 10012

Boil-proof colors can be obtained on cotton and cellulose fabrics through the more time-consuming process with special reactive dyes, obtainable from:

I. C. I. /ORGANICS/INC.
P. O. Box 1274
151 South Street
Stamford, Connecticut 06904

BECKERS
Sveavägen 42
Stockholm, Sweden

Request instruction pamphlet.

Fabrics

Finely woven fabrics like muslin, batiste, percale, etc. are easy to work with. Some dyes, however, do not prove quite color-fast, especially on cotton. In such cases the article may have to be dry cleaned at all times.

Silks are wonderful, though rather costly for the start.

Heavy silks, brocades, and velvets look stunning in batik, but all wax applied to these materials has to be removed in the dry cleaning process.

Man-made or synthetic fibers, such as rayon, dacron, nylon etc. are not suitable for batik, at least not for the techniques described in this book. They only accept special dyes after lengthy and tedious chemical treatments.

Drip-dry cotton, taffeta, some heavy satins, and any coarsely woven materials are also unsuitable for batik.

The finer and closer the weave of any fabric, the easier it will be to work with.

Practically all newly purchased fabrics contain a certain amount of sizing which may prevent the wax and the dye from seeping into the cloth, and might cause patches of uneven coloring.

Therefore, first wash and pre-shrink all fabrics.

And if the chosen material should be colored, it is advisable to boil it for a few minutes and rinse well, to make absolutely certain that all loose color, or dye, has been removed.

It seems a nuisance to have to wash and dry that new material when you are so eager to apply your design. But until you are more experienced in the field, you might as well follow the rules and make sure that the first project does not end in disappointment.

28 'The Owls'

Once we have formulated our idea and jotted it down on paper, cut the material to the required shape. If the material is for a blouse, dress, handbag, or lampshade, we can emphasize the originality of the article by confining the design to the shape of the article. This way we do not waste time decorating inside seams, which would be the case in selvage-to-selvage decoration. Needless to say, it is much easier to work with smaller pieces of material.

When the fabric has been washed, dried, and ironed, it is ready for the application of the design.

For a one-color batik, first sketch your design on paper the same size as the intended batik, then pierce the lines with a pin or tracing wheel. Place the paper over the material and rub fine charcoal dust through the perforations. The design will show on the fabric in a series of little dots. When the fabric is dipped in dye, these dots will disappear completely.

When contemplating a two-or-more color scheme it is preferable to have the design traced in pencil so that the original design will withstand the repeated dyeings. The easiest way to do this is to place the design under the fabric and hold it against a window, and trace the design in delicate pencil lines.

When I am sure of the layout, I draw directly on the fabric. Quite often I start by merely sketching the outlines on the fabric, then developing the design with each waxing. By this I do not mean, that I simply start on a batik with only a ghost of an idea— I just leave the design open to changes or improvements and therefore keep the pencil lines to a minimum.

Some pencil lines have the tendency to survive the most rigorous cleaning methods, so I suggest the pencil be of soft lead, and the lines quite delicate.

Applying the Design

29 'Alhambra'

The Wax

30 *'Giraffes'*

A wax combination of six parts beeswax and four parts white paraffin wax will produce excellent results, or even equal proportions are satisfactory. The lower the percentage of beeswax, the more prominent a crackle will emerge. It is not advisable to reduce the beeswax content to less than 30%.

For any sections of the design where no crackle is desired, the use of pure beeswax, melted with a grain of rosin, is recommended. The rosin ensures that the wax will adhere firmly to the fabric.

To heat the wax to the desired consistency, I suggest a thermostat-controlled hotplate or frying pan. If this is not available a double boiler is excellent, and will eliminate the danger of the brush bristles heating and curling. Also it is a lot safer from the fire hazard point of view.

A plain gas burner or an alcohol lamp with an adjustable burner can be substituted for either.

Do not use a kerosene stove—it will blacken you and your utensiles.

Applying the Wax

When applying the wax design it is necessary to have the fabric in a flat position. Placing the material on a flat surface such as a pane of glass, wax-paper, or a sheet of formica is not satisfactory as the melted wax is inclined to cool quickly on contact with the slick surface and you will also find the fabric adhering to the underlying medium.

My preference is for the material to be pinned to some type of frame. This could be the family clothes horse, an old picture frame, or a professional stretcher. By pinning the material to the stretcher we avoid direct contact with any other surface, and the cloth can be well saturated with the wax from the waxing tool.

Batik is a resist technique, which means that under every drop of wax we are preserving some color, and protecting it against the next. Unfortunately, this is true for any accidental drop. Practically nothing will remove it succesfully, and a spilled or dripped area might well upset the whole design. To avoid this, always squeeze out excess wax against the side of the pan before applying your design.

If we follow the traditional way of using the tjanting, we can use the frames mentioned above, or even pin the material on the back of a chair, as the Javanese woman demonstrates in Plate 16. To apply the wax we have the choice of two types of implements: the traditional tjantings, which come in various shapes and sizes as shown in the illustration of p. 26, or brushes of various widths.

In the West the brush is more commonly used.

For a start I would suggest a set of three flat brushes of 1/8", 1/2", and 1" widths, and preferably of sable, camel hair, or ox bristle. Naturally, the finest brush is for delicate brushwork and the widest brush for covering large areas.

I have seen some craftsmen working with just one medium-size brush which they trim to a wedge. The easiest way to copy this method is to dip the brush in melted wax, let it cool, then cut the bristles diagonally with scissors. A brush of this kind will have a greater capacity for holding the wax, and by manipulation, the point can be used for waxing fine lines, or larger areas can be covered by utilising the full slant of the brush.

Under no circumstances must any drop of water get into the wax pot, as it will spatter.

31 *Trimming the brush*

With the fabric stretched or draped in front of us, we place the wax container just a few inches away, and heat the wax to at least 170°.

32 'Sunflowers'

When applied to the fabric, the wax should be translucent. If it appears to be sitting on the surface, the wax has not penetrated the material sufficiently.

The first time we immerse the brush into the hot wax, the bristles will be inclined to 'fan'. When this happens, gradually press out the air and moisture against the side of the pan until the brush assumes its normal shape.

Carefully load your brush with the molten wax and apply to the fabric in even strokes. According to the design, the brush strokes will be long and even, or short daubs to cover small areas.

As the wax makes contact with the fabric it should be absorbed immediately. If the wax 'sits' on the material the wax is not hot enough, or you are too slow in application, causing the wax to start 'jelling' on the brush.

As we go along we will find that the hot wax has a tendency to run and overshoot the border lines. Control this by keeping the waxing tool at a respectful distance within the border, and letting the wax slowly penetrate to the border line. Experience will dictate the degree of distance.

If you are using the tjanting, hold the container in your hand, exactly if you were holding a dinner knife (Fig. 16, 17, 18 and 20).

It has to be kept at an even level, tilting back the spout in transit from pan to batik, to avoid spilling. Once in a while the spout of the tjanting will clot; so keep a piece of thin wire handy to clear the passage.

After the completion of your first batik, you might find that the brush stroke remains visible. To compensate for this next time, wax both sides of the fabric, particularly if the material has a heavy or coarse weave.

A light brush stroke will allow the minimum of color to seep into the fabric when dyed, and will produce a feeling of restlessness which may serve to emphasize the mood of a design.

Always be careful in your work. A batik that has been waxed has to be handled gently to avoid cracking the wax and causing crackle. Never fold an unfinished batik; hang it in a place where it cannot be disturbed.

The Dyes

Most batik dyes are available in powder form, to be mixed with hot water according to directions. After the powder has dissolved completely, add more warm water until the right shade and strength of color has been obtained, and until there is sufficient liquid to allow the fabric to float freely.

Unless the dye package should advise differently, always add vinegar or salt for either animal or vegetable fibers.

> For dyeing silks or animal fibers, add 2 tablespoons of vinegar (acetic acid 28%) to 1 gallon of liquid, or $1\frac{1}{2}$ teaspoons to the quart. If the vinegar proves too strong and changes the color, substitute tartaric or oxalic acid in the same proportion.
>
> For dyeing cottons or vegetable fibers, add 1 tablespoon of common salt to 1 gallon of liquid, or 1 teaspoon to the quart.

For the beginner who is experimenting, RIT or Tintex dyes are satisfactory, and are available at most supermarkets and department stores. Most aniline dyes can be re-used several times before losing their dyeing power. Therefore, store excess dye solution in labeled bottles for future use.

For the dyeing process it is handy to have a long cover-all or

33 'Klee Town'

apron, and rubber gloves. Also necessary is a vessel large enough to allow the material to float freely. This can be a plastic or enamel bowl or tub, a wooden or copper vat, or a galvanized iron bucket. In the case of galvanized containers, the acid in the dye solution might eat into the metal if left too long.

Aniline dyes, batik wax, stretchers, tjantings, and brushes can be obtained from:

CRAFTOOLS INC., & ALJO MFG CO.
1 *Industrial Road*
Wood-Ridge, New Jersey 07075

Color Mixing

PRIMARY COLORS:

Red

Blue

Yellow

SECONDARY COLORS:

Orange	composed of:	yellow	red
Green	” ” :	yellow	blue
Purple	” ” :	red	blue

TERTIARY COLORS:

Gold	composed of:	yellow	orange	blue
Blue-brown	” ” :	red	green	blue
Red-brown	” ” :	yellow	purple	red
Orange-brown	” ” :	green	orange	red
Bronze	” ” :	orange	blue	purple
Green-brown	” ” :	green	yellow	purple
Brown	” ” :	red	green	
Black	” ” :	purple	green	

34 *Batik pillow. Leaf design*

62.6° Fahrenheit equals 17° Centigrade
64.4　　,,　　　　,,　　18　　　,,
66.2　　,,　　　　,,　　19　　　,,
68.0　　,,　　　　,,　.20　　　,,
69.8　　,,　　　　,,　　21　　　,,
71.6　　,,　　　　,,　　22　　　,,
73.4　　,,　　　　,,　　23　　　,,
75.2　　,,　　　　,,　　24　　　,,
·77.0　　,,　　　　,,　　25　　　,,
78.8　　,,　　　　,,　　26　　　,,
80.6　　,,　　　　,,　　27　　　,,
82.4　　,,　　　　,,　　28　　　,,
84.2　　,,　　　　,,　　29　　　,,
86.0　　,,　　　　,,　　30　　　,,
87.8　　,,　　　　,,　　31　　　,,
89.6　　,,　　　　,,　　32　　　,,
(Heat limit of dye solution for paraffin)
91.4　　,,　　　　,,　　33　　　,,
93.2　　,,　　　　,,　　34　　　,,
95.0　　,,　　　　,,　　35　　　,,
96.8　　,,　　　　,,　　36　　　,,
98.6　　,,　　　　,,　　37　　　,,
100.4　　,,　　　　,,　　38　　　,,
102.2　　,,　　　　,,　　39　　　,,
104.0　　,,　　　　,,　　40　　　,,
105.8　　,,　　　　,,　　41　　　,,
107.6　　,,　　　　,,　　42　　　,,
109.4　　,,　　　　,,　　43　　　,,
(Heat limit of dye solution for pure beeswax)

Wax should be heated to at least 170°F.

Conversion Table
for Dye Solution

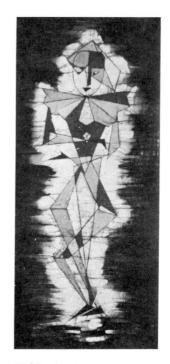

35 *'Firedance'*

Dyeing the Fabric

To me, the dyeing is the most exciting part of the whole batik process. We immerse a rather dull-looking piece of material covered in wax in the dye bath, and when we take it out we recognize the waxed design against the new color. Nothing can be done now to change the brush stroke; the color has penetrated deep into the cloth and there it stays for good.

If you have designed for a one-color project, keep an eye on the effects of contrast against the original color of the fabric. If this is off-white or cream, try black, brown, blue, red, or green, to provide dramatic tonal contrast.

In a multi-color project we are dealing with nuances of colors which in turn create different moods pertaining to the laws of color mixing. Some color combinations do not harmonise with the stark white of bleached fabrics. To avoid such discords, the fabric should be dyed in a light tint before applying the first coat of wax.

When you have decided on your choice of color, prepare the dye according to instructions, taking into consideration the type of wax used on the material.

Pure beeswax will withstand a dye bath of up to 110°F. before melting, wheras paraffin wax must not be immersed in a solution warmer than 90°F.

We must keep these temperatures constantly in mind for all dyeing procedures because the hotter the solution, the faster the dyed color.

While the dye bath is being prepared, lay the waxed fabric in lukewarm water. This will ensure an even and immediate saturation when dipped in the solution.

As soon as the dye bath has the required temperature, stir well, and slowly immerse the waxed fabric and a small test-strip of the same material. Move about very gently to avoid streaks or patches. If crackle is required the stirring can be more vigorous.

36 Batik pillow. Kite design

46

Also keep a piece of paper handy for jotting down relative quantities of water and dye, temperature, etc. for record purposes.

Keep in mind that a color when wet fades a shade lighter when dry. In case of doubt remove the pieces early. The fabric can always be re-dyed if the color is too pale.

After removing the material, rinse the batik in lukewarm water and hang to dry. Rinsing in cold water will cause excessive crackle.

Attach the fabric to a clothesline so that it hangs straight, as shown in the illustration.

37 *Correct hanging method*

Crackle

To quote the *Encyclopedia Britannica* (Edition 1957), "Crackle is an accidental texture which can be governed by the artist only with difficulty. Therefore, though it is perfectly characteristic of this art, it should not be made use of indiscriminately, and the best artists avoid it almost entirely."

It is true that in some Javanese batiks the crackle is hardly visible, yet those delicate veins, giving the impression of marble, are the characteristic of the craft and are a factor that gives an individuality to each piece of batik. Whether it be accidental or willfully produced, it can be extremely effective in some instances, and in others it can ruin the batik. Various temperatures, acids, and the craftsman's hand can cause or avoid it.

Large areas of one shade or areas of undesirable brightness can gain tremendously by the restless mood of a prominent crackle, whereas a delicate design can be spoiled with too much crackle.

Apart from rinsing the batik in very cold water, crushing it in the palms, or pulling it over a finger, we can add and underline the design of a batik by scratching in the wax with a nail or a tooth-

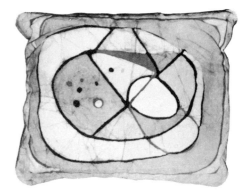

38 *Batik pillow. Abstract design*

39 *Batik pillow. Hieroglyphic design*

pick to cause crackle. Maud Rydin uses the latter technique extremely effectively, as can be seen in some of her work represented in this book. Scratching—or might we call it engraving?—often gives the appearance of stitchery.

At times I have experimented with cookie cutters. I heated the forms on a hotplate and with tongs or a pair of pliers pressed them into the wax. The batik itself I placed on blotting paper to absorb the melting wax. Naturally, the heat of the forms has to be tested on scrap material to be sure they will not scorch.

Any willfully induced crackle or "scratching" has to be applied *before the last* color bath. Since in the last color bath all of the fabric except the darkest color areas are covered by wax, all but the darkest color will show crackle.

Removing the Wax

The majority of the wax on the material can be removed by ironing. The material is placed between layers of paper towels or blank newspaper. As the wax melts under the applied heat, it will be absorbed by the paper. Keep on replacing the saturated paper with fresh layers, until all the wax is absorbed.

This ironing should be done extensively since the heat of the iron is a helpful agent in fastening the textile color.

To protect the ironing board against grease marks, cover with several layers of newspaper.

In Indonesia and other countries where I have seen batik being done on a larger scale, the wax is removed in a way to enable reuse. This of course, is not possible when ironing out the wax.

If the colors in a batik are fast, the fabric can be immersed in boiling water, and the molten wax skimmed off the top. Wax gained by this method can be re-used for waxing dark colors.

Another method of saving wax is to construct a thermo-tray, illustrated here. Once the wax in the batik starts to melt, it is gently removed with a scraper. This calls for caution in heating, as an over-heated tray might singe the material.

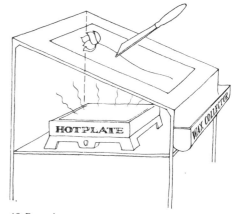

40 *Removing wax*

In the case of a wall hanging or screen, the batik is complete. But wearing apparel, pillowcases, or any article that has to be cleaned of even the last bit of wax still left in the fabric will have to be dry cleaned. For a silk dress or blouse, I recommend professional dry cleaners, but for many items the cleaning process can be done at home by soaking and rinsing the batik in a bath of white gasoline, or a mixture of two parts gasoline and one part turpentine. There are also many dry cleaning fluids available under various trade names.

When the batik is immersed in the cleaning fluid the wax will dissolve. The cleaning fluid should be renewed several times until all wax is removed. Toward the end of this procedure the fluid will be fairly clean, and can be stored for future use.

However, extreme caution should be excercised when using cleaning fluid as it is extremely inflammable. Never work near an open fire, and make sure the room is well ventilated as the fumes can be poisonous.

Incidentally, if your local dry cleaners are equipped with a steam box, roll your batik in paper towels and steam for two hours at 200°F. This will affix the dye permanently.

Dry Cleaning the Batik

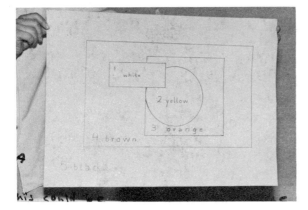

(a) Draw design on fabric

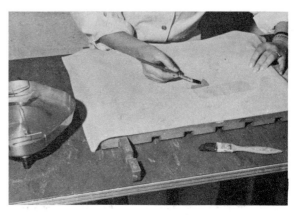

(b) Apply the wax

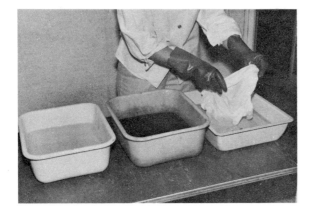

(c) Immerse in lukewarm water

(d) Dip in dye solution

41 *Step-by-step dyeing method*

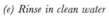

(e) Rinse in clean water

(f) Crush before final dyeing to obtain crackle

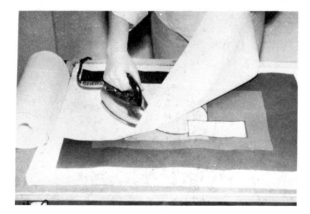

(g) Remove wax by ironing between paper

Step-by-Step
Dyeing
Method

Chart for a multi-colored batik

WHITE

[a] Wax over all parts of the design that are to remain white.

YELLOW

[b] Soak fabric in lukewarm water and immerse in yellow dye. Rinse and hang to dry.

ORANGE

[c] Soak fabric, and immerse in red dye. Rinse and hang to dry.

BROWN

[d] Soak fabric, and immerse in brown dye. Rinse and hang to dry.

BLACK

[e] Soak fabric, and immerse in black dye. Rinse and hang to dry.

[f] Iron batiked fabric between sheets of paper to remove wax. Dry-clean if the fabric must be completely free of wax.

All wax applied to the fabric at various stages remains until the end, unless a new color scale is imposed. This is only recommended for advanced craftsmen.

Some aniline dyes can be used several times within a period of a few weeks before they lose dyeing power. Therefore, store the dye solution in labeled bottles for future use.

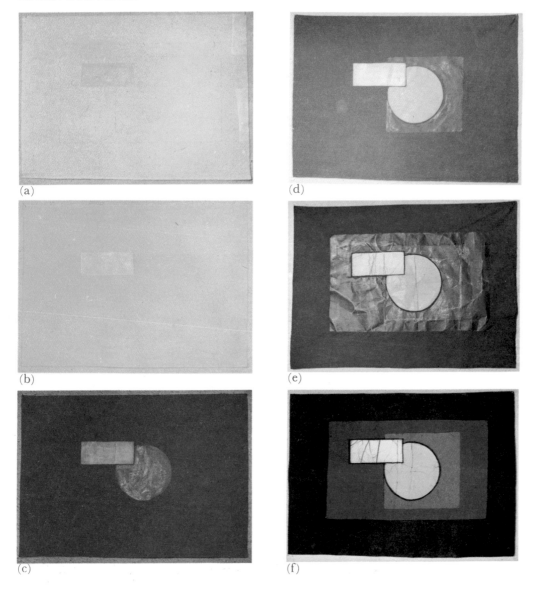

(a)

(b)

(c)

(d)

(e)

(f)

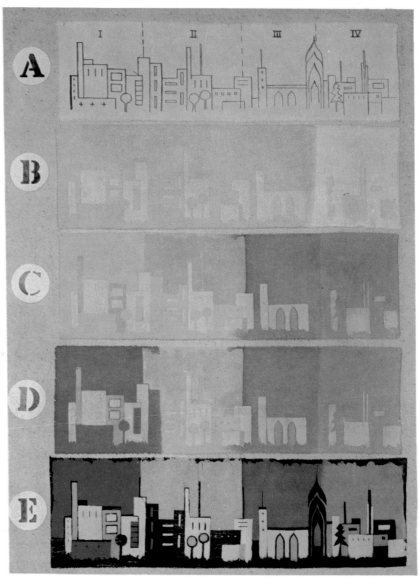

43 *Color sequence*
for sectional dyeing

The time will come when we feel too restricted by the laws of color mixing, perhaps because a design calls for a strong contrasting color. To obtain this, we have the following possibilities.

We can remove all the wax and impose a new scale of colors next to and over the already existing one, rewaxing only the parts that we definitely want to keep in the present shade. This is the way the Indonesians do it.

The wax can also be removed in parts with a dry cleaning fluid, consisting of two parts gasoline and one part turpentine. Before applying the second color scale, the batik would only require some touching up with wax along the edges of the newly freed areas.

We could try out some "sectional dyeing," which means that the batik is only partially immersed in the dye. It calls for careful handling to prevent the dye from splashing onto the section which we want to preserve for a another color.

The dye can also be applied with a brush. For that purpose batik dyes may prove to be too weak, while silk-screen or textile-

Sectional Dyeing

44 *Sectional dyeing. Step (d)*

45 *Scratching lines with an empty ballpoint*

[a] Wax all parts that are to remain white.

[b] Immerse section I, II, and III in yellow. Wax all parts that are to remain yellow.

[c] Immerse sections III and IV in blue. Wax all parts that are to remain blue or green.

[d] Immerse section I in red. Wax all parts that are to remain orange.

[e] Immerse the whole batik in black.

Sectional
Dyeing
Procedure

printing colors would produce better results. In either case, we are really moving away from the authenitc batik, and rarely will we achieve the harmony or unity that make a good batik. We do, however, produce contrast, and some artists combine the silk-screen technique, block-printing, stenciling, and stitchery with batik.

In painting, printing, or stenciling on the textile color, the pigments are often applied too thickly and boldly so that they do not blend in with the rather muted tones of a real batik.

Tie-Dyeing

Tie-dye is not really batik. It requires no waxing at all, but the dyeing procedures are the same as in batik, in that the lightest shade is dyed first. Due to this similarity of technique, the two can be co-ordinated with stunning results, especially on wearing apparel—tie-dyeing being the first step and batik the second. (Rolf Hartung, in his recent book *More Creative Textile Design,* explains and illustrates tie-dyeing in detail.) The possibilities of this technique are manifold and again leave a wide margin for experimentation and imagination. Tie-dyeing has the great advantage of allowing the material to be immersed in boiling hot dye solutions.

In tie-dyeing we tie thread or waxed string tightly around a small piece of the white fabric in one of the ways demonstrated in the illustrations. With the strings or threads all tied, throw the fabric into a dye bath, then rinse and dry it. When the threads are removed the fabric has remained white where we had tied the threads. The results will look like plates 47, 48, and 52.

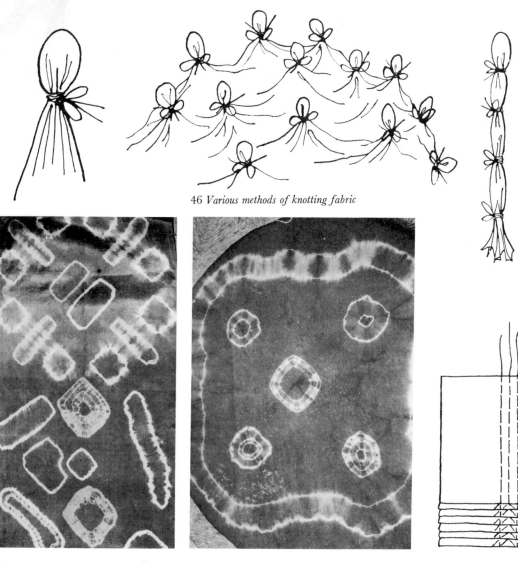

46 *Various methods of knotting fabric*

47 *Sample of tie dyeing*

48 *Section of tie dyed cushion*

49 *Running-stitch method*

50 *Tieing the fabric*

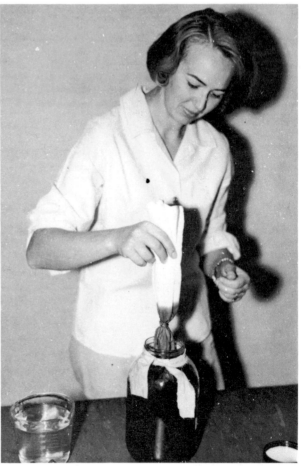

51 *Dipping in dye solution*

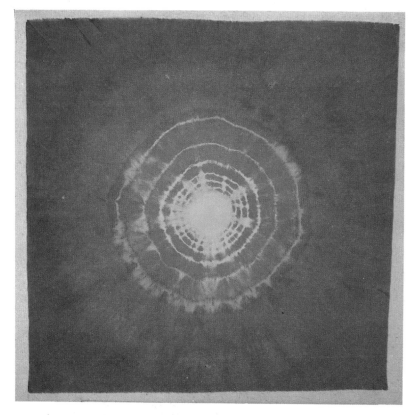

52 'And then there was light . . .'

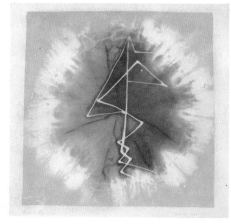

53 'Man in the Moon'

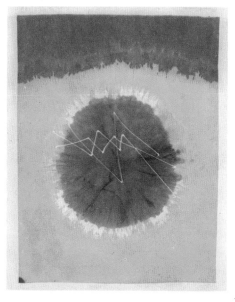

54 'Sound Barrier'

55 *'Still Life'*

56 *'Desert Mirage'*

57 *'Memory of a Clown'*

58 *'The Clash'*

I used to frown on the idea of keeping records of my work, and I am sure many craftsmen feel the same way. Nonetheless the day will come when you produce a color combination which you like particularly well, and unless you have the phenomenal capacity of remembering what fabric you used, what dye, how much of it, how long you immersed it and at what temperature, you will most likely fail to reproduce the same color. Petty as it sounds, we do learn a great deal from these statistics.

When a batik is completed, attach the test strip to a card giving all information. This will represent a comprehensive record of each batik, and in this way we teach ourselves more than we could learn from any amount of lecturing.

Keeping a Record

NAME OF BATIK _____

SIZE _____

TYPE OF MATERIAL _____

Sample Chart

	dyes used	*quantity*	*temp.*	*time*	*setting agent*	*colour obtained & other comments:*
1st dip	pink	$\frac{1}{2}$ oz. + 1 gal.	78°F	10 min.	1 tbsp. salt	delicate pink
2nd ,,	lemon yellow	1 ,, + 1 ,,	78°F	30 ,,	,,	orange-yellow
3rd ,,	scarlet	1 ,, + 1 ,,	78°F	30 ,,	,,	bright scarlet
4th ,,	black	1 ,, + 1 ,,	76°F	40 ,,	,,	jet black

Modern
Batiks

59 *Batik by Maud Rydin*

60 'Bird Tree'

61 Batik by Maud Rydin

62 *'Homer City'*

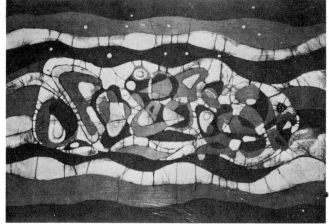

63 *'Pebbles'*

64 *'Forest Fire'*

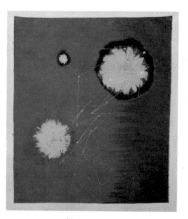

65 *'Oddball Atom'*

66 *'Inferno'*

67 *Cotton blouse* 'Squares'

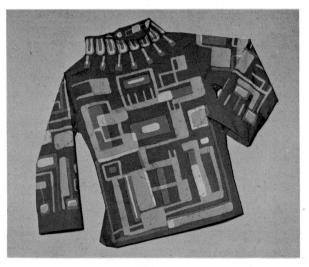

68 *Cotton blouse* 'Upsala'

69 *Cotton blouse and hat* '**Athens**'

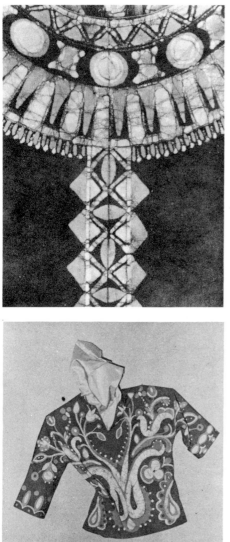

70 *Detail of batik on velvet by Maja Lindroth*

71 *Cotton blouse 'Jitterbug'*

72 *Cotton blouse 'Pennsylvania'*

73 *Batik by Greta Digman*

74 *'Smoke Rings'*

75 *Batik by Alice Wedel*

76 'Sailboats'

77 Batik drapery by Maja Lindroth

78 'Widow'

80 *'Contemplation'*

81 *'Divided Town'*

79 *'Ode to Ella'*

82 *Batik by Nils Wedel*

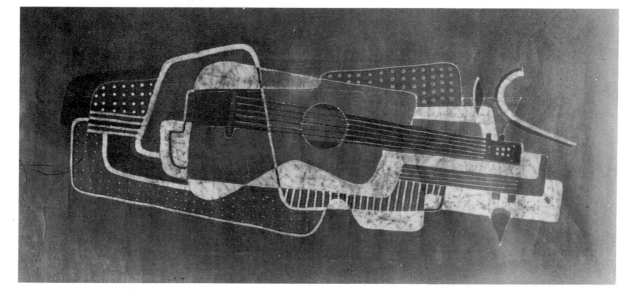

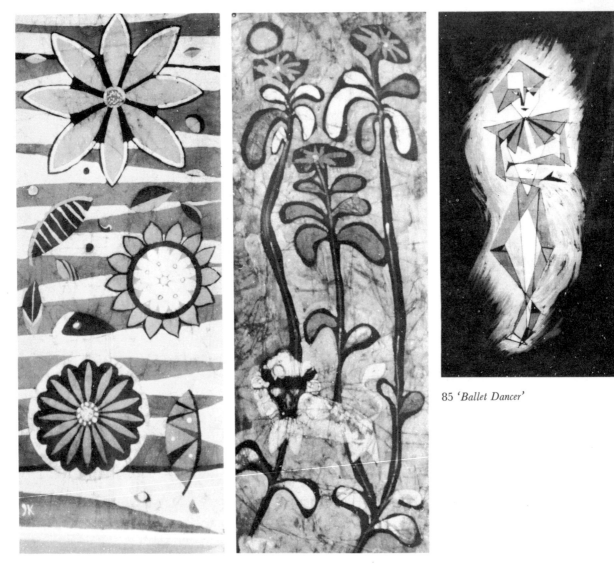

83 *Flower panel*

84 *Batik by Jodi Robbin*

85 '*Ballet Dancer*'

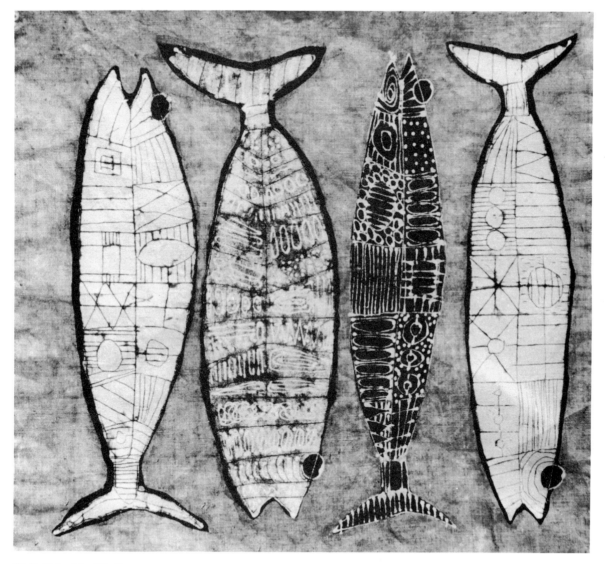

86 *Batik by Maud Rydin*

87 *Batik dresses by Maja Lindroth*

88 *Batik blouse by Maja Lindroth*

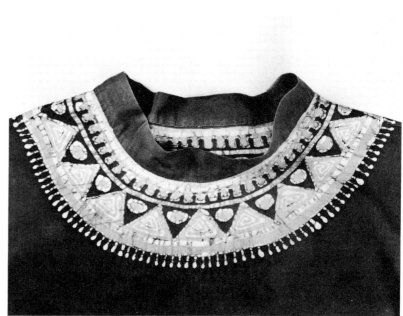

89 *Detail of neckline*

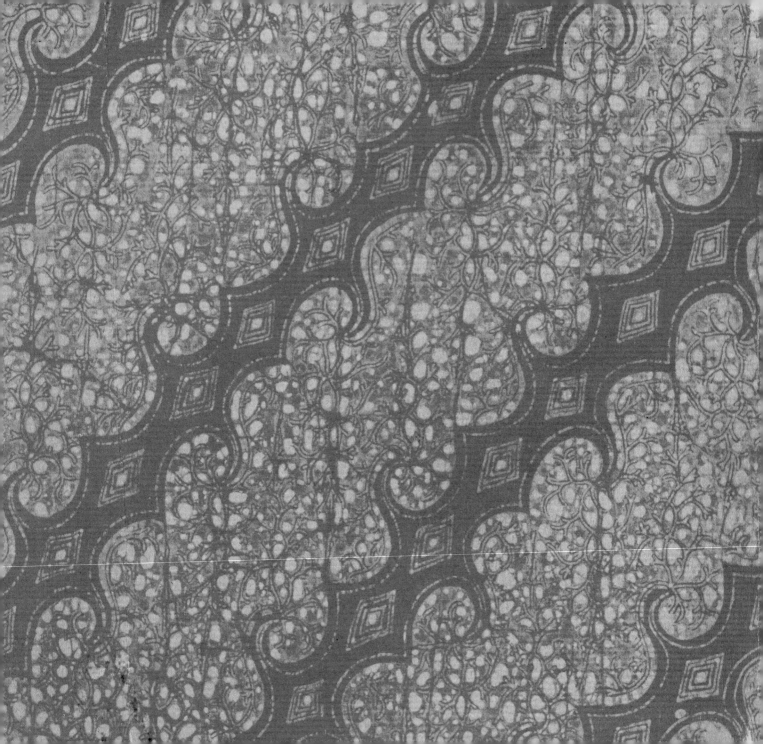